Ruling

Your Days

Like Clay Under a Seal

BRIAN D. ECHEVARRIA

Ruling
Your Days
Like Clay Under a Seal

© 2012 Brian D. Echevarria

ISBN: 0983699127
ISBN-13: 978-0-9836991-2-5

website: JLIConnect.com
Email: info@JLIConnect.com

Unless otherwise indicated all scriptures are quoted from the *King James Version* of the Holy Bible.

Printed in the U.S.A.

DEDICATION

To Jesus Christ my Lord, King, and God.

RULING YOUR DAYS

CONTENTS

ACKNOWLEDGMENTS

I would like to acknowledge Dr. Elizabeth Hairston-Mcburroughs, Dr. D.K. Olukoya, and Dr. Onyebuchi Daniel. Their teachings have influenced me through mentorship or literature in this endeavor.

INTRODUCTION

Prayer, intercession, and spiritual warfare are very important in the life of every believer and to the establishment of the kingdom of God on earth. Over the years I have had the opportunity to experience the many graces of God in prayer, intercession, and spiritual warfare. In sharing these with others, I have discovered that many do not experience the fullness of what God has for them in the area of prayer. This is really a negative situation because prayer is the entryway to intercession and effectiveness in spiritual warfare. If many have not experienced the fullness of God in prayer, even fewer have experienced any level of effectiveness and success in intercession and spiritual warfare.

Intercession may be one of the most important ways through which we interact with God. Jesus Christ Himself lives to make intercession for us.

> *Wherefore he is able also to save them to the uttermost that come unto God by him, seeing he ever liveth to make intercession for them.*
>
> *Hebrews 7:25*

His very existence is an act of coming between us and our Holy God. It is unthinkable that so many Christians who aspire to be like Jesus Christ have never really pursued the grace of intercession—something He is constantly doing.

Everything we have been delivered and healed from and forgiven of has been attained through the intercession of Jesus Christ. How then it is that Christians would neglect this? The neglect of intercession has been a major trick of the enemy.

Intercession is the act of coming between parties with the intention of reconciling those who differ or contend. When we go to God pleading on behalf of another, it is an act of intercession. Many have unwittingly done this for people they love or have concerns for. When we intercede to God, we bring a petition on behalf of one who is weak and needs our help, or we simply feel led to pray. This can also be prompted in us in a few different ways. Sometimes people ask for prayer. At other times you see people and you know they need intercession. Still at other times, people share their circumstances and you volunteer to pray for them. Perhaps, like Jesus, the Father shares that someone's faith is going to be sifted by Satan and you take it upon yourself to pray, or intercede, that their faith does not fail them. All of these things are possible beginnings to the act of interceding to God.

There is another aspect of intercession that is greatly ignored in the church, which is the act of interceding against the enemy. When Jesus Christ said that the gates of hell will not prevail against the church, in a most basic sense, He meant that there was an offense happening on the part of the church. The church would be imposing His will against hell and hell's gates would not be able to withstand it. To intercede also means to come against the enemy on behalf of another. This can be done in a very rude sense, without invitation as many prayer warriors already know. There may be, or have been, times when the enemy was having his way with someone you know and love and you took it upon yourself to come against his work. This aspect of intercession should only be as you are more and more sure that it is the will of the Lord.

In the Old Testament, the root word for *intercession* is translated in various ways such as "to meet, fall upon, to strike, to cut down, or to have laid upon."[i] All of these biblical expressions are seen as a part of what it means to intercede. In the Bible, we have Samuel falling upon and striking the Amalekite king, Jacob meeting with the Angel of the Lord, Moses, Daniel and Ezra praying for the children of Israel, and the most perfect form of intercession in our Lord Jesus Christ having our very sins laid upon Himself. With these few examples we see that intercession and its fullness embodies many different dynamics and covers nearly every area of life.

One dynamic of intercession, which we must not ignore, is spiritual warfare.

In general, there are four levels of spiritual warfare. The first level is in the heart and mind of every human being. This is where people battle satanic thoughts and fight to believe. The god of this world, Satan, blinds the minds of those who do not believe.

A second level is what many refer to as ground-level warfare. At this level believers in Jesus Christ, through the authority of His name, cast demons out of people and places. It is beyond debate that the church has a duty to do this because it is one of the signs that follow those who believe.

And these signs shall follow them that believe; In my name shall they cast out devils; they shall speak with new tongues;

Mark 16:17

Another example of this is Jesus Christ declaring that He saw Satan fall like lightning as the people He sent were doing ground-level warfare.

And the seventy returned again with joy, saying, Lord, even the devils are subject unto us through thy name. And he said unto them, I beheld Satan as lightning fall from heaven.

Luke 10:17-18

Many have wrongly interpreted this as Jesus Christ witnessing the fall of Satan when he rebelled, but a closer look at text brings the understanding that the ground-level warfare and strategic-level warfare, which is the third level, complement one another.

Strategic-level or high-level warfare happens in the heavens. A great example of strategic level warfare can be found in the book of Daniel when he was waiting for an answer from God and the Angel Gabriel was held up in the heavens by an evil prince. In the book of Judges, you find Deborah talking about the stars aligning in their courses and in Thessalonians, Paul disclosing that Satan withstood him when he wanted to return to Thessalonica.

They fought from heaven; the stars in their courses fought against Sisera.

Judges 5:20

Wherefore we would have come unto you, even I Paul, once and again; but Satan hindered us.

1 Thessalonians 2:18

Perhaps another great example of Jesus doing strategic-level warfare would be when He rebuked the waves and the wind of the great storm. Satan made an attempt on Jesus' life just as he did to destroy Job's possessions and family.

And there arose a great storm of wind, and the waves beat into the ship, so that it was now full…And he arose, and rebuked the wind, and said unto the sea, Peace, be still. And the wind ceased, and there was a great calm.

Mark 4:37-39

A fourth level of spiritual warfare is the occult level. This is the place where agents of Satan are engaged for the wickedness they perpetuate on the earth through witchcraft. This is perhaps the most overtly aggressive offense of the enemy against many individuals, families, and societies. Paul had an encounter at the occult level with a sorcerer named Elymas.

But Elymas the sorcerer (for so is his name by interpretation) withstood them, seeking to turn away the deputy from the faith. Then Saul, (who also is called Paul,) filled with the Holy Ghost, set his eyes on him. And said, O full of all subtilty and all mischief, thou child of the devil, thou enemy of all righteousness, wilt thou not cease to pervert the right ways of the Lord? And now, behold, the hand of the Lord is upon thee, and thou shalt be blind, not seeing the sun for a season. And immediately there fell on him a mist and a darkness; and he went about seeking some to lead him by the hand.

Acts 13:8-11

Believe it or not, there are people who willing give themselves over to opposing the King and His kingdom here on earth. You can rest assured that, like Paul, there are times when God's answer to them is you.

Ruling Your Days will briefly address the areas of strategic-level and occult-level warfare. Both of these topics are vast, so we will concentrate on dealing with designs in the heavens that are in place, and being placed, to covertly rule your day to day affairs. This book has been written primarily for people who have already taken the School of Intercession with me through Jesus Life International or have a basic foundation of prayer and intercession.

The most important factor when engaging in any of the things of the spirit is to have the character of Jesus Christ flowing through your life. The difference between you and the agents of Satan is not power but the character of Jesus Christ and submission to God. If those things are not in place, before long, the enemy will turn you into one of his agents and you will find yourself doing his will as an enemy of God.

As you turn the pages of this book, there may be things that you have not seen, do not agree with or understand, or grip you with fear from the enemy. What we all must do is believe the word of God and be led by the Holy Spirit as we submit ourselves to the pursuit of the truth. In any case it is necessary for one to be humble and teachable to learn anything new, including this.

I look forward to you ruling your days like clay under a seal.

RULING YOUR DAYS

CHAPTER 1

When we consider the fact that much of what God has for us involves our participation in order to obtain it, we must take into account our responsibility to intercede and do warfare for ourselves and others. Many times it would seem that the responsibility to do this simply relies on nice prayers being brought before heaven. Intercession and warfare include aggressive responses and proactive declarations and actions in order to be most effective.

Let us take a look at a few words because agreement can very well fall apart at the point of differing definitions.

When we consider the meaning of intercession and the reason it needs to be done, the word intercede is very important. Webster's defines *intercede* as "to interpose in behalf of someone, as by pleading or petition…to attempt to reconcile differences between two people or groups; mediate."[ii] With this definition, we understand that intercession is not something that we do for ourselves but something we do on behalf of others to God. To mediate is to be interposed between two parties at variance with the view of reconciliation being a possibility.[iii]

The most remarkable of all the translations is "to be laid upon." I find it to be the most remarkable because this is the form of intercession that brought salvation from God.

This is what is spoken of in the book of Isaiah when it says that our transgressions were laid upon Jesus.

> *All we like sheep have gone astray; we have turned every one to his own way; and the Lord hath laid on him the iniquity of us all.*

> *Isaiah 53:6*

Jesus Christ went to the Father on our behalf and not on behalf of Himself. The other definitions of intercession, however, give us a more full-bodied view as to what it is to intercede. It means to meet for reconciliation, light upon to take from one place to another, fall upon, strike, cut down, and to hit the mark With all of these different meanings of what it is to intercede, we can conclude that intercession can be quite rude in the sense that you must barge into certain situations in order to bring peace between the two parties. Intercession can also be quite aggressive in that you must fall upon attack and cut down what the enemy is doing against another.

As we discuss what it is to deal in the heavens and shape the day, we must maturely understand why this must be done. You and I have a destiny fulfilled in Christ, a good work that He has prepared beforehand that we should walk in. There are three main reasons that we pray and intercede: relationship, maintenance, and establishment. Most if not all of our prayer will fall under one of these three categories. We pray and intercede because we are given the opportunity to participate in something with Jesus. He lives to intercede for us and invites us into that work. This is a wonderful way to nurture and grow our relationship with Jesus Christ. Through prayer and intercession we must maintain what we have gained and accomplished so that the enemy is unable to take back or ruin the things we have gained in anyway. The great majority of what we behold with our eyes in the world today is a result of prayer or the lack thereof. Also through prayer and intercession, we establish the kingdom and will of God right here on earth as God responds to what He has put in our hearts to pray.

It is important to note that when one begins to deal with the heavens, command the morning, and shape the day like clay, one must have a pure heart. The second you begin to declare your own will into the heavens, you have made yourself no different than those who serve Satan and declare their own will into the heavens. When the Bible tells us that God searches the heart and knows its thoughts and intents that should inspire tremendous fear concerning the reason we do things. No matter how much we paint the outside of the sepulcher, the inside is full of dead men's bones and God knows that. Perhaps you would be able to fool the religious and perhaps you would even be able to deceive yourself, but surely you will be unable to fool the Lord. Be humble and honest before you implement these powerful spiritual truths in your life.

In spiritual warfare and deliverance, we have to fight for everything we obtain, including our daily walk with the Lord. We must fight for the Word and we must fight to keep it in our hearts. We fight to get it, we fight to keep it, and we fight to pass it on. This is simply the life of a child of God.

The whole time that we are fighting these battles in intercession and spiritual warfare, we are also completely in love with God. Though we are wide open for more love and never looking for more war, they are both happening at the same time—love and war. So many times different communities of believers get caught up in one aspect of the kingdom. You have one community deemed as the spiritual warfare camp because they walk in authority and dominion, and you have another community deemed the glory camp because they walk in the glory of God. I believe that those two rivers are coming together and that we are those people who walk in the glory of God and still exercise authority and dominion.

King David is a great picture of one who worshiped God and killed the enemy. I find that to be pretty neat. Worshipping God did not keep him from being aggressive in establishing the kingdom Israel was promised and fighting to establish the kingdom did not keep him from being tenderhearted in worshiping God. We do not have to be one or the other, which represents our own expression—the expression of our souls. When we tap into the spirit man that is absolutely in love with God and ready to expand His Kingdom, we have no problem walking as both worshiper and warrior. We love people and we stop for that one person in need yet we cast out devils. We clothe the naked and we pull down strongholds. We sit and listen lovingly to people and we bind principalities. Do we have to choose one or the other? No. We have the time and nature for both! We are eternal beings so time is on our side. I am eternal. You are eternal. We are supernatural. We are believers—the very image of

God, the house of God, where His name dwells. We are the "baddest" of God's creation.

RULING YOUR DAYS

CHAPTER 2

There are some things concerning the heavens that we need to tap into and speak to because nations are shifting, lives are changing, destinies must be fulfilled, and disciples need to be made. Do you know why Greece has had so many problems in the past few years and perhaps beyond? To the natural man, it may sound ridiculous but it stems from years of intercessors coming against Greek, or linear, thinking that wars against the word of God and its deliberate application. It wars against our ability to simply tap into faith. Now, as a nation, some of the decisions have not been well thought out. Through the years, Christians have shaken the nations through intercession and there is a spiritual war over that nation and what it represents in the spirit realm and historically.

You cannot believe and analyze at the same time; it is impossible. You have a responsibility to study later, but you must believe now. The Bible says,

> *"...Ye shall not see me, until the time come when ye shall say, Blessed is he that cometh in the name of the Lord."*

> *Luke 13:35*

That is the difference between the United States and some other nations; they believe. There is not a different God; they believe. In the west, everyone is a scholar trying to check the theological doctrine as someone preaches. I have a doctrine, His name is Jesus. Ultimately, everything we do and teach must point right to Him. If that is the case we are probably on track with the Bible someway, somehow.

We complicate things and it prevents us from just walking in faith. Understanding is not a precursor to obedience. Some of the things I am going to say you are not going to understand right away, but I am telling you, if you obey, you will get the results.

> *"If any man will do his will, he shall know of the doctrine, whether it be of God…"*

> *John 7:17*

In many cases with God, understanding comes way after the doing. Just ask Zechariah, who did not have a chance to speak. He began to question God and God silenced him. Why? Because all he had to do was believe and obey; just agree. It is the doers of the word who are justified.

Concerning every corporate fast in the Bible, it only took one person who the people were submitted to, to hear. Some of us say, "I just don't feel led by God." If you don't feel led, feel told. God did not have to check with the people to see if they had plans that weekend. You know us, "Yes, I was going to fast but my wife's birthday is this weekend, so I just don't feel led." No! How about you just feel told. We are fasting. Why? Because God is going to do something for us and you are included in that number. Now go ahead and pull your weight in this cause because everyone has something going on that can produce a conflict with their involvement with a number of spiritual things.

I was introduced, by fire, to some of the heavenly things that I understand and in the midst of it all I learned. I had to obey before I understood. That is what you call training. There were some things that happened to me and because I had the right training and bore the character of a son of God, intercession and spiritual warfare was my automatic response. Some, who know me, know that I am a little more militant in my faith. I'll hit you in your mouth about Jesus before my mama because what you say about my mama might be true. She is loved but not perfect. We all love our parents but they are not perfect people. You have to get personal about Jesus. Why? You are son or daughter who stands to inherit this heavenly kingdom. You are not a hireling. The kingdom of God is not business to me but personal. I am all in and fully vested in this. This is my inheritance and it is your inheritance. Get fully vested because this should be very personal to you as well. A lot of the questions that we have about how we are going to work out this life that we want to live, which is but for a moment, are simply questions about where we are vested in the kingdom. I am saying one way—full speed, Jesus. You must be all in to have a realistic expectation of favorable biblical results.

Sometimes as Christians we feel as though we have options as to what we will implement in our personal lives. With so much to be applied it is easy to believe that one thing or the other is not necessary for our success. When it comes to faith in the word of God, we must have faith in the whole word of God if our intention is to the see the promised result realized. It is understandable that certain aspects of the word are more spiritual than us and therefore difficult to receive. Even the apostle Peter expressed difficulty in understand certain writings of Paul.

> *And count the patience of our Lord as salvation, just as our beloved brother Paul also wrote to you according to the wisdom given him, as he does in all his letters when he speaks in them of these matters. There are some things in them that are hard to understand, which the ignorant and unstable twist to their own destruction, as they do the other Scriptures.*
>
> *2 Peter 3:15-16*

In this wonderful ascent to spiritual dominance on behalf of the kingdom of God in every aspect of your life, you will have to apply faith in things that are difficult to understand and obey at times when you are uncertain as to why. Let's take a look at a scripture that may very well be difficult to understand though certain things are plainly stated.

> *And God said, Let there be lights in the firmament of the heaven to divide the day from the night; and let them be for signs, and for seasons, and for days, and years:*
>
> *Genesis 1:14*

Okay, what are the lights for? Their purpose is for signs, seasons, days and years. In Job, God mentioned the Mazzaroth and in Deuteronomy He says,

> *And lest thou lift up thine eyes unto heaven, and when thou seest the sun, and the moon, and the stars, even all the host of heaven, shouldest be driven to worship them, and serve them, which the Lord thy God hath divided unto all nations under the whole heaven.*
>
> *Deuteronomy 4:19*

Do not look at the stars lest you be compelled to worship them. Why? He put them there so they may tell a story. The magicians saw through the stars that Jesus was born. Those stars were telling the truth, and God says, "Hey, my people, you do not look at that."

At this point, take a moment and declare: I renounce, right now, my zodiac sign, in the name of Jesus.

Horoscopes and everything surrounding it are speaking something. It may very well be useless if somebody is just figuring out what they are going to write in a magazine or publication. Regardless, leave that stuff alone! Half of the church says, "You know, none of that stuff is real." No, it is absolutely real. God said in His word that the lights are up there for signs. They are telling a story.

> *And let them be for lights in the firmament of the heaven to give light upon the earth: and it was so.*
>
> *Genesis 1:15*

"And let them be," meaning in addition to those things let them also be for lights on the earth.

> And God made two great lights; the greater light to rule the day, and the lesser light to rule the night: he made the stars also. And God set them in the firmament of the heaven to give light upon the earth, And to rule over the day and over the night, and to divide the light from the darkness: and God saw that it was good. And the evening and the morning were the fourth day.

Genesis 1:16-19

Now, there is something unique because God created the sun and the moon to give light. Then God says, "And," which means "in addition to." We have a problem with the "and." We want the sun to be only this beautiful light during the day that we play in and the moon to be only a stunning light at night. There are witches and wizards worshipping the moon. Do you think they do it because nothing happens? Of course something is happening. God warned you that you too would be compelled to worship the sun and moon if you lifted up your eyes and set your affections to them.

The key in Genesis 1:16-19 is God said, "Let them rule…" or have dominion. This messes with our doctrine a bit. God placed this authority with the sun and the moon. He is the initiator of authority and Satan perverts and counterfeits authority. This being true, we must never forget that God is the initiator of authority. He said let them have dominion. Let them have authority in the day and authority in the night. Not the lesser lights but the greater lights: the sun and the moon.

You do not have to understand right away. I want you to, but first I want you to follow simple instructions as you read through this book. I want you to obey because what we now understand is that those things literally have dominion over our head and authority in our lives. Why? Because God gave the sun and the moon dominion to rule over the day and night and we live in both the day and the night.

As we consider what it is to have faith and obedience in our life we must also have faith that God has done what He has done and given authority to who, or what, He has given it to. Many young Christians understand that faith without works is dead. If one says they have faith they must have a corresponding action that activates that faith and proves its existence. Abraham believed God concerning the promise made to him that his children would become a mighty nation. He proved that he believed God's promise to the point that he was willing to sacrifice his son Isaac at God's instruction, even though it was in Isaac where the promise of God rested. Had he not climbed the mountain and placed his son on the altar of sacrifice, there would have been no way to prove that his faith even existed. That is where we are today; we are in the place of faith that gives evidence through our actions. The Word of God is to be considered for its content, what is it saying, and acted upon. Nothing in there is in vain, not even statements about the sun and the moon.

You can accept the mysteries that we steward and enjoy their benefits.

CHAPTER 3

We as believers have greater authority, but since most of us do not want to touch the full measure of that authority, the sun and moon get to do whatever someone else tells them to do. Ask yourself: who is ruling the heavens over my head? That is what we are dealing with here.

Thou shalt not be afraid for the terror by night; nor for the arrow that flieth by day; Nor for the pestilence that walketh in darkness; nor for the destruction that wasteth at noonday. A thousand shall fall at thy side, and ten thousand at thy right hand; but it shall not come nigh thee. Only with thine eyes shalt thou behold and see the reward of the wicked.

Psalm 91:5-8

Have you ever stopped for a moment to consider that the things listed were actually what would strike down the thousands and the ten thousands? We have quoted this scripture over and over again in our personal devotion but many times we never stop to consider what it is that would strike down a thousand and ten thousand but would not come near us.

The Lord is thy keeper: the Lord is thy shade upon thy right hand. The sun shall not smite thee by day, nor the moon by night. The Lord shall preserve thee from all evil: he shall preserve thy soul. The Lord shall preserve thy going out and thy coming in from this time forth, and even for evermore.

Psalm 121:5-8

It is interesting to me that somehow God believes that we would need protection from the moon. The sun is easy to rationalize because one could get sunburned or perhaps dehydrated. However, the moon has no physical effect that we would need protection from. What could it be?

These are the types of powers the church has not stood against—powers that literally chase us down and influence our daily affairs to the point of causing failure, sickness, or even death.

Hast thou commanded the morning since thy days; and caused the dayspring to know his place;

Job 38:12

You may rightly be thinking that whether we wake up or never wake up again in life the dawn is going to be the dawn and it is going to be in the right place. So what is the Lord talking about? We talk about place when we talk about authority. We say, "Hey, you need to know your place." God is saying, "Make the dawn know where it belongs." But He is not talking about where it belongs physically because that was already programmed when He made the evening and the morning. God is not talking about whether the dawn needs help knowing when to rise and give light. That was in the beginning before man was made. The dawn already knew it had to appear every single day. He is saying, "Have you caused the dawn to know its place, or are you going to let it rule over your head? Whoever is ruling it will rule over your head." The Hebrew meaning of the word *place* in this verse is actually translated as "standing condition."[iv] We must cause all of creation to know where it stands concerning us.

Unfavorably agents of Satan like witches, wizards, sorcerers, and such are far more committed than most Christians. They fast, pray, and have a slave-like mentality. They are prepared to commit an act of sin or unrighteousness at a moment's notice. Paul adopted a slave-like mentality. The one who talked about us being led and being the church of God referred to himself as a bond servant of Christ. He fully understood that, in addition to his simple childhood in Christ, he was also a slave of Jesus Christ. There is nothing wrong with being a slave of Jesus Christ; He is not a cruel Master at all. Since I have been born again, I have never been abused by God. Many times we try to choose what we are to God. Are we friends or are we children? Are we sons or are we slaves? We are both and all. Many ask, "Well, how can we be both? I don't understand."

Declare and tell your day: I am a believer.

The Word says I am a friend. I believe it. It says I am a child. I believe it. The Word says I am an heir. I believe it. It says I am a servant. I believe it.

We do not have to choose. We are not abandoning our sonship because we accept that He has also said that we are servants. We are not abandoning our servant hood because He has also said that we are heirs. We are not abandoning anything. Hey, it says it and I believe it. Stop trying to pick sides on the Word and just believe everything. You read it, believe it. That's it.

Though it asks in Job 38:12, "Hast thou commanded the morning since thy days; and caused the dayspring to know his place…" consider the next verse.

> *That it might take hold of the ends of the earth, that the wicked might be shaken out of it?*

> *Job 38:13*

Out of what? Out of the earth? No! He is talking about shaking the wicked out of the heavens. Can we shake them out of the heavens, the place that is ruling over the earth? Yes, thus they are shaken out of the earth.

In addition to simply giving light, the sun and moon rule by day and by night. He clearly said, "I'm going to put them there to give light and to rule." If He would have only said "to rule," then somebody would have said, "Well, that just meant give light." He had to make Himself clear because He knew that we would debate the Bible and carnal men would spend generations trying to remove supernatural and spiritual aspects of it. He said the sun and moon are going to give light and they are going to rule. It was not one or the other; they were going to do both of those things.

Now, I want to know if you have commanded the morning since your days and caused it to know its place? The agents of darkness rule over the heads of men on earth from the heavens.

It is turned as clay to the seal; and they stand as a garment. And from the wicked their light is withholden, and the high arm shall be broken.

Job 38:14-15

Well, we know that He is not talking about the light of day because He causes the sun to shine on the righteous and the wicked. He is not talking about withholding the sunlight from the wicked. He is talking about doing warfare against the witches, warlocks, wizards, magicians, sorcerers, prognosticators, forecasters, and whatever job or title they have. It is that the light be withheld from them. This means the wicked will not be able to see what is going on in the heavens concerning your life; they will have no divination.

I want to make known to you a ministry called Prayer Mountain—intercessors who pray at 5:00 AM. The idea is to give the day shape because it takes form like clay under a seal. They believe the scriptures! In times when official letters were sent, clay was put on an envelope and stamped to seal it. The more exposure that clay gets to air and heat, the harder it becomes. The seal cannot be changed without the clay being broken. In other words, who has given your day shape? It takes the form like clay under a seal. The further the day goes along, the more difficult it is for you to change the form it has been given as a seal, no matter how much authority you think you have. Have you commanded the morning since your days? Have you caused the dawn to know its place? As you put it in its place, it is not going to rule over your head, but it will declare the glory of God in your life.

We must come to the realization that the worlds were framed by the word of God and that through that same word God placed all the works of His hands under the dominion of mankind. Every single day is waiting to be given orders as to what should take place in it. The sun and the moon are being ruled by a man somewhere over your head. Why shouldn't that man be a good Christian man with the kingdom of God and desires of Jesus Christ at the forefront of his mind? This case is proven through the exploits of Joshua.

> *Then spake Joshua to the Lord in the day when the Lord delivered up the Amorites before the children of Israel, and he said in the sight of Israel, Sun, stand thou still upon Gibeon; and thou, Moon, in the valley of Ajalon. And the sun stood still, and the moon stayed, until the people had avenged themselves upon their enemies. Is not this written in the book of Jasher? So the sun stood still in the midst of heaven, and hasted not to go down about a whole day. And there was no day like that before it or after it, that the Lord hearkened unto the voice of a man: for the Lord fought for Israel.*

> *Joshua 10:12-14*

Joshua spoke to the sun and the moon and gave them physical instructions as to where they were to be. The Lord gave him special authority that day to speak even contrary to the orders that the sun and the moon had been given previously in regards to their rising and setting. I have always found it interesting that the Bible declares that God hearkened unto the voice of a man but never says that Joshua was praying to God regarding that. Joshua spoke directly to the sun and the moon and God placed an authority with him that caused the sun and the moon to alter their position.

Declare and tell your day: every design placed in the heavens by wicked programmers, I dismantle you in the name of Jesus.

Tell the sun, "I rose before you and I am telling you what you are going to do today." Why? Because we have dominion and Jesus made it clear.

Have you commanded the morning since your days and caused it to take shape like clay under a seal? Through faith in the Scriptures, you should now know that you walk in a level of authority that reaches even to the heavens. There are things there that are in our favor because God created them for us as His children. However, Satan has been busy raising his own children and, through our ignorance, they have hijacked the heavens in many ways. The powers that strike down the thousands and ten thousands is really subject to your authority as a child of God. I believe it is time that you take that authority and use it to give every day shape like clay under a seal. Prayer Mountain is a prayer ministry that proves that well-trained believers are unstoppable. You with the authority of God are unstoppable and no wicked agent can hinder you in the heavens.

Like Joshua, it is time for you to rise up in faith and take authority so that every battle is won in your favor. The Amorites discovered that there was no escaping the servant of God who was exercising dominion in the heavens and the agents of Satan in our day will discover the same as we apply the name of Jesus in the heavens as well.

CHAPTER 4

*And Jesus came and spake unto them, saying, **All** power is given unto me in heaven and in earth.*

Matthew 28:18 (emphasis added)

Go therefore. We have dominion in the heavens and the earth. With the above statement Jesus was declaring the expanse of His kingdom.   A king's name only carries authority within the boundaries of his dominion and with persons who are subject to him when outside of his dominion. This fact makes what Jesus said so powerful. He has dominion EVERYWHERE!

Wherever we speak the name of Jesus, something is going to happen. When people say Christians do not have the authority to speak in the heavens, they are not downgrading the authority of the believer. They are downgrading the authority and effectiveness of the name of Jesus. The name of Jesus will work if they put me on a space shuttle and send me to the farthest galaxy known. It will work scuba diving off the coast of Florida or shooting down a portal in Antarctica. It will work in the heavens over the place I reside.   The name of Jesus will work wherever it is spoken. Hallelujah to the Most High God!

It is written in Job that the day takes form like clay under a seal.   However, I have to take authority before the sun starts doing its thing.

Declare: Let every program in the heavens placed by wicked agents, concerning me, be changed, in the name of Jesus.

> *The heavens declare the glory of God; and the firmament sheweth his handywork. Day unto day uttereth speech, and night unto night sheweth knowledge. There is no speech nor language, where their voice is not heard. Their line is gone out through all the earth, and their words to the end of the world. In them hath he set a tabernacle for the sun, Which is as a bridegroom coming out of his chamber, and rejoiceth as a strong man to run a race.*

> *Psalm 19:1-5*

The scripture refers to the sun and the moon and reveals that there lines would go to the end of the earth. There is no place where their voice is not heard. In other words, if you learn to speak in the heavens, you can touch somebody in Thailand. There is no place where their voice is not heard!

From this passage we can see that the day and night have a voice that is heard everywhere and the sun behaves as a strong man. We have the opportunity to no longer be smitten by the words and powers in the heavens but to rule our days in the name of Jesus. That is why we need to grow up in all things concerning the Lord. We are so busy asking for the city when God said to ask for nations.

> *Ask of me, and I shall give thee the heathen for thine inheritance, and the uttermost parts of the earth for thy possession.*

Psalm 2:8

I am asking for nations because God said that I can. I am asking for nations because Jesus said to make disciples of *all* nations, baptizing them in the name of the Father, the Son, and the Holy Spirit. It is time for us to stop eating the crumbs on the floor like those who do not have a covenant with God. If Jesus commanded us to make disciples of all nations and the word of God tells us to ask for the nations, why should we continue to ask for the crumbs of nations, which are cities?

Say: God, give me the nations.

You can speak over those nations if you learn how to get in the heavens, but you have to get up. At the break of dawn things begin to change immediately. If you and I are in any kind of contract negotiations and I beat you awake, while you snooze and let the sun rise, you lose before you even take a shower that morning. Why? Because I am going to give the day form like clay under a seal. You say, "Well, I like to have my quiet time around 7:00 AM. I sit with coffee at the table and I have the beautiful sunlight." You might have a great time with Jesus, but you may have lost many things in your day already.

Declare: In the name of Jesus, let every power trying to capture my days fall.

I am teaching you how to war for your days. This is what you declare in the early mornings and by 7:00 AM your victory is already sealed. How? Because we know the rules and the laws to God's government. He asked in Job 38:33, "Knowest thou the ordinances of heaven? canst thou set the dominion thereof in the earth?" Eventually our answer to that question needs to be yes.

He put things in the heavens with a real purpose. He did not put them up there as vain decoration. We need intercessors who will rise early in the morning. Now, some of us say, "But it's just so early." Well I have had some early flights and I have had to be at the airport by five o'clock in the morning, and somehow, I woke up and caught my flight. It is all about what is important to you. It is about making a decision and putting value on something. That's what it's about. "Well, I'm tired." You caught your flight at 5:00 AM. "Things are going on. I've got so much on my plate. I don't know if I can keep on praying." You caught your flight at 5:00 AM. You thought you were having a rough time before you started praying, stop commanding the morning and watch what happens. You already beat back a lot of what the enemy wanted to do. Do not sleep in without discerning that it is a time to rest. We have to get rough in prayer and disturb all those witches, their plans and places of worship.

There is something called an altar. An altar is a place of worship, sacrifice, and communion with a deity. Many Christians do not know that we have an altar. However, the scriptures plainly state that we dor.

> *We have an altar from which those who serve the tent have no right to eat.*
>
> *Hebrews 13:10*

Though we may not realize it, as priest of God, all of our dealings are before the altar of Calvary. The place of the greatest sacrifice of God's son, the Lamb of God, is the place that we have our communion, worship, and make sacrifice to our God.

This is not only true for Christians, it is also true for anyone dealing with any spiritual entity. Agents of Satan must establish spiritual and sometimes natural altars to deal with the different demons they are serving. It is at their altars that satanic priests establish their plans against the children of God and the kingdom of Jesus Christ. Through the name of Jesus, we must take authority over the works that they establish at their altars wherever their altars may be—whether in the heavens, under the waters, or in the living room. An altar is a spiritual place that can be reached easily with declarations.

Declare: I take authority over every altar established against myself, my family and the ministry within a 25-mile radius of this place in the name of Jesus. I disgrace the priest attending those altars in the name of Jesus.

All children of God can do it. It is not because I am a super apostle, preacher, or teacher; it is because I am a believer who has the name of Jesus and I know the laws of His government regarding this matter. The day must take form as clay under a seal and light must be withheld from the wicked. I meet people all the time that are divining against me and maybe not even on purpose; but through Christ, I fix that.

Declare: I take authority over every third eye peeking into my life in the name of Jesus. Let the arrows of the Lord pierce you through, right now, in the name of

Jesus. I take authority over every witch and I say repent or die.

Thou shalt not suffer a witch to live.

Exodus 22:18

Repent or perish are the laws all of us have, but a witch who decides to continue in their practice, that is their business. If God wants to save them, that's fine, but I have marching orders. Many in the occult have gotten saved, that means God had mercy on them. Chances are when they were serving the devil—if they were doing something with real apostles and prophets in an area—those apostle and prophets were working to take them out just like they were trying to do the same. Our heritage is to execute the written judgment. People say, "Well, you've got to have compassion." I do, but I have real compassion. I do not have false compassion that leads us to condone wickedness.

To execute upon them the judgment written: this honour have all his saints. Praise ye the Lord.

Psalms 149:9

Everybody wants someone nice and sensitive until the doors in their house start rattling. Then they want somebody strong to come over and get rough with darkness. You want me to speak to you in "love" until your kids are having nightmares. Then, all of a sudden, you want a warrior in your house, you want me throwing oil against the wall. A few minutes earlier you thought I was speaking too roughly. Now you want me to come and wrestle with principalities and powers. Wrestling is an active thing. It is our heritage to have what we say, but sometimes we say it at the wrong time of day and it is just too late.

We can have what we say but we should say it at 5:30 am instead of 8:30 am. The difference between the priesthood in the Old Testament and that in the New Testament is very vast, but the New Testament priests carried swords. Glory to God! We have weapons of our warfare that are not carnal but mighty through God. When we speak in the name of Jesus, something is going to shift.

We hope we shift it correctly because sometimes we miss God. That is why the Bible specifically says that none of Samuel's words hit the ground; God was not worried about His own words hitting the ground. There is a difference between our words and God's words. When you speak in the name of Jesus, you cannot say, "Oops, I made a mistake, so that's not going to be obeyed." No, if we speak in the name of Jesus, it will be obeyed. That is why we have to give accounts of our stewardship—how we used the authority that we have been given. He is not itemizing it trying to see what authority He is going to let us have at what moment for each thing. No, if the authority is ours, it is ours.

When the angel was to lead Israel, God said to Moses, "Beware of him, and obey his voice, provoke him not; for he will not pardon your transgressions: for my name is in him" (Exodus 23:21). He did not say, "Look, if he decides not to pardon you, I'm going to pull him aside, talk to him and change that decision." No, he can use the authority given to him and he will give an account for the way he used it. That is you. It is time for us to stop wasting our inheritance by snoozing. Why? Because God gave dominion to man, not Christians. If a mere man is taking authority over your days and you are not, your days will obey the mere man—meaning the witch, the warlock, the prognosticator, the sorcerer, the magician.

Many times there is a design in the heavens that you need to discover and tear down. We do not even know that these designs are in the heavens because we are so busy listening to everybody say "your battle is in your mind." That is one of the battles we are fighting and our mind is one of the warfronts. There are also battles in the heavens, underneath the waters and underneath the earth, and we have authority everywhere the battles take us. But we are not going to fight a battle we are denying is going on.

In Judges 4 and 5, you have the story of Deborah and Barak. There was a warlord and this man was greatly feared. He tormented Israel and his hour had come. He did not understand why his army was getting defeated. God's providence just dominated the situation. He ran from the battle and into the tent of a woman named Jael. Now, can you imagine how scared she must have been though there was peace between Sisera's king and her husband? I know we paint her like a warrior, and she did do a warrior action, but let's look at the reality. She knew about this warlord Sisera. He was mean, he was a murderer, and he came into her tent. She was scared but there was something she had to do.

Deborah then sang a song about what had occurred! Whenever God's people got a victory, they sang a song exalting the Lord and what He had done to the devil. Here it is: they defeat Sisera and she wrote a whole song about it. That is what we need to do. We need to get to the place where we break out into praise when God brings the victory. Do you know how embarrassing that is? They had a whole song about someone getting whipped. Deborah sang,

They fought from heaven; the stars in their courses fought against Sisera.

Judges 5:20

They fought from the heavens. Who? The stars in their courses fought against Sisera. That word *stars* can also be translated as "princes." That's amazing. They chose to translate it into English as "stars," but it said the princes fought from the heavens. That battle was won in the heavens, not in Jael's tent. That was already handled early in the morning hours; Sisera was going down! Somebody gave that day a form and he was going to fall, whether on the battlefield or in the tent of a woman.

And she sent and called Barak the son of Abinoam out of Kedeshnaphtali, and said unto him, Hath not the Lord God of Israel commanded, saying, Go and draw toward mount Tabor, and take with thee ten thousand men of the children of Naphtali and of the children of Zebulun? And I will draw unto thee to the river Kishon Sisera, the captain of Jabin's army, with his chariots and his multitude; and I will deliver him into thine hand. And Barak said unto her, If thou wilt go with me, then I will go: but if thou wilt not go with me, then I will not go. And she said, I will surely go with thee: notwithstanding the journey that thou takest shall not be for thine honour; for the Lord shall sell Sisera into the hand of a woman. And Deborah arose, and went with Barak to Kedesh.

Judges 4:6-9

But we know that Deborah said the glory would go to a woman. She prophesied what was determined in the heavens. She said, "Look Barak, you need to know that you are going to do this but a woman is going to get the glory." It had been arranged in the heavens. It might have been personal for Deborah. I look at those things. Deborah might have said, "See this Sisera, he has been mocking us. He's been treating us badly, talking about 'how they have a female leader. How can a female be a prophet and judge?'" There's no telling what Sisera was saying. "A female prophet? Oh, please." Deborah said, "Oh, okay. I've got something for him. I'm going to deal with the heavens. I'm going to put the dawn in its place and shake the wickedness out. I'm going to make sure that light is withheld from those witches and occult powers that are supporting Sisera. I'm going to shake him out of the heavens and make sure that he is disgraced; a woman will get the glory for defeating him. I will shape this day like clay under a seal."

It is simple authority; just read the whole story. You have got to figure that there is a narrative going on. Deborah was not disconnected from Sisera, she was at war with him in the book of Judges. They fought from heaven. They fought against Sisera. It was determined in the heavens that Sisera was going down.

> *Blessed above women shall Jael the wife of Heber the Kenite be, blessed shall she be above women in the tent. He asked water, and she gave him milk; she brought forth butter in a lordly dish. She put her hand to the nail, and her right hand to the workmen's hammer; and with the hammer she smote Sisera, she smote off his head, when she had pierced and stricken through his temples. At her feet he bowed, he fell, he lay down: at her feet he bowed, he fell: where he bowed, there he fell down dead.*

> *Judges 5:24-27*

Here is this woman who pounded Sisera and put a peg through his head. That is adrenaline; she was scared. It is called fight or flight. That is what I perceive happened and she chose to fight. She put a peg through this man's head and she knew she had only one chance because it was Sisera. "If he gets up, I'm dead." She had to make it count and so do you.

The dominion that Jesus passed on to the church reaches all the way to the heavens. When Jesus stated that all power had been given to Him in heaven and earth, that was exactly what He meant. As a servant of God you are equipped with authority in the name of Jesus to make declarations that shake every power of darkness that is coming against you and the kingdom of God. Whether that altar is in the heavens or on the earth, you can rest assured that the name of Jesus will bring forth a mighty blow to the enemy. Every declaration and design that they fashion against you will come to nothing at the use of the authority that God has given you through Jesus Christ. Even death is swallowed up in victory.

CHAPTER 5

If you get up, begin taking authority and giving the day its form, you will look like a juggernaut in the spirit in just a few weeks. Your life will shift. Now the enemy is going to come back. Those people who were not use to you fighting will be shocked that you began fighting. You will catch them off guard and they are going to fight back when they realize what has happened. It will take persistence because you have the greater authority, but you have to use it. You might start out twice in one week and you are thinking, "Yeah! I'm walking in victory." All of a sudden, you have to be up every morning because that is where the battle has gone.

And in the morning, rising up a great while before day, he went out, and departed into a solitary place, and there prayed.

Mark 1:35

Jesus believed in getting up early, before the sun, and praying. It was a part of what He did. There are some things that are only going to be done before the sun rises. Walk the day in, stand guard, stand watch. Watching is to sleeping as fasting is to eating. We have to watch! It is going to cost you a little sleep. You might feel a bit physically exhausted the next day, but you will get used to it; just take a nap.

You can rule, proclaim the will of God, and command the heavens to line up with the prophetic declaration of God.

Declare: I throw out everything that these wicked people have programmed into you, heavens. Morning, I impregnate your womb.

The Bible says in Psalm 110:3 that the morning has a womb.

Declare: I impregnate the womb of the morning with the Word of God, with breakthrough, with victory. I lock out every contract trying to bid against mine, right now, in the name of Jesus. I set up a design and decree that this is what God has for me, and I lock it out, right now. I say that every power trying to come against this contract I'm putting down will fail because this is the will of God.

People will just start changing their minds when the demonic programming is removed, if it is the will of God. The witches who want to frustrate you by driving up the price of a house will be stopped. Consider this: God promised you a house. You put in a bid and somebody else comes and outbids you on that same house. Now you are paying $60,000 more because you would not wake up and rule your day like clay under a seal. They did nothing but the devil's will. They came to rob you of your money just by bidding. They stole by putting bids in and made you pay more for what you knew God promised. If God promised you, and you know it is the will of God, why not get up in the morning and defend it?

Declare: In the name of Jesus, I tear up every contract, every note, and every insinuation written against me. Right now, I set a design in the heavens according to the Word of the Lord that when my enemies come against me they will stumble and fall.

If you do not, they will come and they will eat you.

Tomorrow morning get up at 4:45 AM. It's like work. You get there a few minutes early to get yourself settled to be praying at 5:00 AM. Just begin to speak to the Lord and He will lead you into the battle.

Declare: Every word programmed against me in the sun and the moon, I blot you out by the blood of Jesus, right now.

Just do it. Get up and do it. Jesus got up before day. In Genesis 14, Abraham took his guys out by night when he was going to get his nephew Lot. He whipped the tail of those who took Lot before the day broke because he understood something. Do you think he just wanted to go out early in the morning? No. He understood that something was going on and he was going to go get the victory. He was going to go get his nephew. By the morning he had the victory. I am telling you that you can have the victory every single morning. You can rule your day and give it form like clay under a seal. You can order your day. Get it done. Come against the witchcraft that has been opposing you from the heavens.

Declare: I break the power of every hex, vex, spell, enchantment, divination, sorcery, and incantation

spoken and hidden in the heavens against me, right now, in the name of Jesus.

I guarantee your adversaries are banking that you will not touch it up there.

Declare: Sun, I command you, in the name of Jesus, to return every affliction meant for me back to the sender seven times worse.

Some will say that it is not right to pray against your adversaries. My answer to that is nothing changes what you believe faster than life. When the enemy has his hands around your neck, then you will want to do warfare. It eventually becomes personal. When he was just messing with your neighbor, no action was necessary. That is because we do not have real love. Why does nothing change with what we believe until we are personally afflicted? We should also war for the brethren—you know the ones who we are bound to by the blood of Jesus. Like Christ died for us, we should also lay down our lives for the brethren. We have all power, all authority in the name of Jesus Christ, by the blood of Jesus Christ.

Whenever we speak and are in our proper place, we have all the power necessary to do what God has sent us to do. This includes beating down any witch, any warlock, any sorcerer, any magician, and any false prophet who wants to speak against us, and what God has commanded us to do.

Now, we have another issue. What do we do about the people who do not know they are operating in witchcraft or any other wickedness? The same thing we do about the people who know. "Well, what if my mama doesn't know she's speaking curses?" Hey, sorry for mama!

Declare: Every curse spoken against me, I return to the sender sevenfold in Jesus' name.

Let the chips fall where they will. What a man sows, he will reap and if you do it to me, you will reap it seven times more. We live by the same rules. We cannot go around cursing people; we do not get to do that. If we do curse people then we get to eat seven times more. People who are laid down, loving God and reading the word can make a difference by just taking authority in the morning. You will see your loved ones get saved as you get beyond yourself and start ruling your day for kingdom affairs. You will see loved ones literally come into the light of the gospel. Why? Because they were caged up in the heavens with some old incantation from somebody. All it takes is somebody like you to get into the heavens and do something about it; but we are sleeping.

In general, we need stay up late or be up early. We can command the morning at 2:00 AM, but if you are dealing with some heavyweights, I suggest dealing with it late night and early morning but make sure you get lots of rest. Tomorrow morning wake up just before five o'clock. You do not have to stay up for the rest of the day. Get up, command your morning, finish at six o'clock and catch a 30-minute nap. Jesus asked His disciples why they could not tarry with Him for one hour.

Ruling your day is not worship time. I know we say worship is warfare but if you are up to bind the devil, bind the devil. Speak with a tone of authority because the heavens are listening and will think you are not serious if you do not. If you get up in the morning and start worshipping and praising God while the principalities and all the arrangements are just waiting to be dismantled, they wait and keep on waiting because all you did was worship God. You never actually did any spiritual warfare. The principalities are like, "Oh, I thought I was going to have to leave." If you are up to tear down the principalities, tear down the principalities.

Ruling your day is love <u>and</u> war. Don't choose but do them both and put them in their rightful place. Let's grow up, let's love God and let's do effective spiritual warfare. We are going to love Him lavishly. We must be all in for God like David. In one breath, he said, "The Lord is my shepherd" (Psalm 23:1), and in the next minute, he said, "He teacheth my hands to war, so that a bow of steel is broken by mine arms" (Psalm 18:34). So can you.

HEART OF AN INTERCESSOR

Intercessor: the unseen portion of the family; a thankless assignment that only receives praise of God; the selfless stance in a relationship with the Lord. This person is not self-seeking or looking for recognition. The honor that comes from the Lord is all the honor this one needs. Many times they are the driving force behind what we see in the natural. Whether for their actions or lack thereof, intercessors are involved in every facet of ministry. The intercessor is one of two people that the word of God declares He is looking for. The Lord is looking for intercessors and worshipers.

> *And I sought for a man among them, that should make up the hedge, and stand in the gap before me for the land, that I should not destroy it: but I found none.*

> *Ezekiel 22:30*

> *But the hour cometh, and now is, when the true worshippers shall worship the Father in spirit and in truth: for the Father seeketh such to worship him.*

> *John 4:23*

Why would the Father be looking for a man to stand in the gap? Why would God Almighty ask someone to stand between Him and the land? Who is this person and why was one not found? What kind of person is this who makes a wall and stands in the gap?

The Father is looking for man to petition Him on behalf of them that will not, cannot, or know not. Many are the transgressions of man against our Holy and Righteous God. Governments and authorities have gone against the ways of the Lord and found themselves in a war that they cannot win. God, because of the righteous, has held back His hand. There are people all over the world standing in the breach between men and God and making a wall of the righteousness and the blood of His Son. He looks for a man to stand in the gap lest He destroy the land. Let's look at Jesus.

Jesus has made intercession and is still making intercession. We know from the word of God that He ever lives to make intercession for us and that He is seated at the right hand of the Father interceding on our behalf. We know that He petitioned the Father for the forgiveness of them that crucified Him on the basis that they knew not what they were doing. We know that He bore the chastisement—stood in the gap—and intercepted what was headed our way. We know that He has stood in the gap between us and the curse of the law. Jesus died so that we would not have to. Jesus, in the gospel according to John, entreated the Father for all them that would come to Him. He prayed to the Father that Peter's faith would not fail Him. He produced true righteousness in the earth through His death, which is what God required to not destroy the land. You see this earlier in the Bible with Abraham's intercession for Sodom. His intercession is still heard today! Bless the Eternal God of Heaven!

The Lord Jesus Christ is the ultimate and complete intercessor. He is filled with such compassion and desire to see the will of the Father done that Isaiah tells us that He made intercession for the unrighteous! While we were yet sinners, Christ died—interceded—for us.

We see here the complete heart and thought of a true intercessor. Jesus was all about what the Father wanted. He came to give the Father what He required on behalf of the world. We see that He is full of compassion for all. We see that His compassion would not lead Him to ask something out of the will of His Father; "...not my will, but thine, be done" (Luke 22:42). These are the words that thrust forth our salvation. The cry of an intercessor on assignment: I will stand where You tell Me to stand, I will ask what You tell me to ask; however You want me to do it, I will do it if it hurts, I will do it if I do not want to. I am on assignment!

To function as an intercessor, we must have the heart of the Father. It is His will that is prayed into the earth. When we know the Lord Jesus Christ, it will lead us to know the Father. In John 14:9, Jesus said "...Have I been so long time with you, and yet hast thou not known me...and how sayest thou then, Show us the Father?" It is in His character and example that we must walk. There must be perfect unity with the Father through the Spirit of God. Jesus was led by the Spirit. Shouldn't we? The Holy Spirit will show us what to pray and intercede for.

For what man knoweth the things of a man, save the spirit of man which is in him? even so the things of God knoweth no man, but the Spirit of God.

1 Corinthians 2:11

May we walk in the vocation that we are called and fulfill the ministry given to us…Jesus did!

Holy Spirit! He comforts, teaches, leads, reminds, convicts, intercedes, shows things to come and knows the will of the Father. Perfect intercession takes place when one yields to Him and brings before the Father what He reveals. God Almighty is interested in what He is interested in at the time. Many wonder where the intimacy with the Lord goes and comes from. It is in the flowing with His Spirit. God only flows one way. That is His way. Intercessors must know this. It is a tough thing to swim up river in the natural. How about the spirit? Let us look at Ezekiel's account of the river of God flowing out of the sanctuary.

Afterward he brought me again unto the door of the house; and, behold, waters issued out from under the threshold of the house eastward: for the forefront of the house stood toward the east, and the waters came down from under from the right side of the house, at the south side of the altar. Then brought he me out of the way of the gate northward, and led me about the way without unto the utter gate by the way that looketh eastward; and, behold, there ran out waters on the right side. And when the man that had the line in his hand went forth eastward, he measured a thousand cubits, and he brought me through the waters; the waters were to the ankles. Again he measured a thousand, and brought me through the waters; the waters were to the knees. Again he measured a thousand, and brought me through; the waters were to the loins. Afterward he measured a thousand; and it was a river that I could not pass over: for the waters were risen, waters to swim in, a river that could not be passed over. And he said unto me, Son of man, hast thou seen this? Then he brought me, and caused me to return to the brink of the river. Now when I had returned, behold, at the bank of the river were very many trees on the one side and on the other. Then said he unto me, These waters issue out toward the east country, and go down into the desert, and go into the sea: which being brought forth into the sea, the waters shall be healed. And it shall come to pass, that every thing that liveth, which moveth, whithersoever the rivers shall come, shall live: and there shall be a very great multitude of fish, because these waters shall come thither: for they shall be healed; and every thing shall live whither the river cometh.

Ezekiel 47:1-9

Please note that the river had a direction that it was flowing. So much so that Ezekiel described the direction four different times in the first two verses of the chapter. Wherever the river flowed everything lived. The intercessor cannot create a flow and give direction to the river. It is already flowing where the Lord wills and intercession is to be made for who, what, and where the Lord will bring life at a particular time.

Intercession is not forcing one's own will into the atmosphere. The intercessor walking with a right spirit will not dare do such a thing. Rather it is petitioning the Lord to do what He has relayed to you that He desires to do. He makes His desires known to them that pray. Whether by His Word, vision, or a by way of a still small voice, it is a must that one who is an intercessor know the will of God. Show us where your river will flow, Lord! Jesus Himself spoke of this saying numerous times in John that He only said what the Father said and did what He saw the Father doing. This would lead one to believe that He only prayed what the Father asked Him to pray. Please notice that I said *asked*. The Lord will make no one pray and intercede. He, by His Spirit, will prompt and lead. It is up to us to respond with reverence and appreciation to the Lord and get on our assignment. Intercession is a privilege considering that there are many who God can call on other than us.

It is my understanding that more people perish than necessary because of lazy and uncommitted intercessors. Imagine if the Lord Jesus Christ was too tired to intercede for us to the Father when He asked that we be with Him where He is. We would be without the first few verses of Ephesians which says that He has "blessed us with all spiritual blessings in heavenly places in Christ" (Ephesians 1:3). What if He took a break and forgot to ask the Father that Peter's faith would not fail him. We would have lost a portion of the New Testament and, worse yet, who would have brought the first fruits of the gentiles to the Lord. Undoubtedly God Almighty would have just picked someone else because His counsel will stand and His word will come to pass. Nevertheless, we see where intercession took place to bring forth what the Father would have to be done. Time would fail us to speak of the intercession of Nehemiah, Solomon, Jeremiah, and the Apostles for each of the churches. David would have had innocent blood on his hands unless Abigail had stepped forward. Israel would have been annihilated unless Moses, through his relationship with Jehovah, humbled himself and interceded for the nation.

And the Lord said unto Moses, I have seen this people, and, behold, it is a stiffnecked people: Now therefore let me alone, that my wrath may wax hot against them, and that I may consume them: and I will make of thee a great nation. And Moses besought the Lord his God, and said, Lord, why doth thy wrath wax hot against thy people, which thou hast brought forth out of the land of Egypt with great power, and with a mighty hand? Wherefore should the Egyptians speak, and say, For mischief did he bring them out, to slay them in the mountains, and to consume them from the face of the earth? Turn from thy fierce wrath, and repent of this evil against thy people. Remember Abraham, Isaac, and Israel, thy servants, to whom thou swarest by thine own self, and saidst unto them, I will multiply your seed as the stars of heaven, and all this land that I have spoken of will I give unto your seed, and they shall inherit it for ever. And the Lord repented of the evil which he thought to do unto his people.

Exodus 32:9-14

And the Lord said unto Moses, How long will this people provoke me? and how long will it be ere they believe me, for all the signs which I have shewed among them? I will smite them with the pestilence, and disinherit them, and will make of thee a greater nation and mightier than they. And Moses said unto the

Lord, Then the Egyptians shall hear it, (for thou broughtest up this people in thy might from among them;) And they will tell it to the inhabitants of this land: for they have heard that thou Lord art among this people, that thou Lord art seen face to face, and that thy cloud standeth over them, and that thou goest before them, by day time in a pillar of a cloud, and in a pillar of fire by night. Now if thou shalt kill all this people as one man, then the nations which have heard the fame of thee will speak, saying, Because the Lord was not able to bring this people into the land which he sware unto them, therefore he hath slain them in the wilderness. And now, I beseech thee, let the power of my lord be great, according as thou hast spoken, saying, The Lord is longsuffering, and of great mercy, forgiving iniquity and transgression, and by no means clearing the guilty, visiting the iniquity of the fathers upon the children unto the third and fourth generation. Pardon, I beseech thee, the iniquity of this people according unto the greatness of thy mercy, and as thou hast forgiven this people, from Egypt even until now.

Numbers 14:11-19

In both of these recorded accounts of Moses making intercession for the people, we see the acceptable will of God to destroy Israel and make a great nation out of Moses. It was His acceptable will, not His perfect will. The heart of the intercessor must be one of humility. Greatness in the acceptable will of God was presented to Moses. Yet the perfect will of the Father was what Moses asked for. Moses was able to humble himself to the will of God and make intercession. Yes, humility comes in when it is time to pray for your church. It sends shock waves through the spirit when intercessors ask only for what is acceptable and not that which is perfect. Example: the pastor is out of order. You believe that you are called to pastor also. Instead of you praying the perfect will of God, in this example—which is to turn the heart of the pastor and bring restoration to that ministry—you ask that God would expose him and you start another church that will be better than the one you currently attend. We must humble ourselves, intercessors. May the perfect will of God be our cry and not just that which is acceptable. Moses, who was not born of the Holy Spirit, was able to choose what was right between the opportunity to be promoted and the restoration of people that God loved. How much more than Moses should we have the ability to make the right decisions when we have been born of the Holy Spirit?

How else could one put aside his thoughts, ideas, and opinions without humility? Can we intercede for someone when we are not willing to agree with God concerning His desires for that person? Are you saying that an intercessor needs to be ready to put aside all of His own opinions and thoughts? Yes. "…not my will, but thine, be done" (Luke 22:42). What a humble statement. Father, I will pray for them that mistreat me and despitefully use me. I will bless them who You desire to bless, regardless of what I feel about them. Not my will, but Your will; You who knows all, sees all, and understands all.

As you begin or continue on this journey into the life that God has empowered you to live, you must not only rule your days but have the right heart while doing it. What are your motives? This book may have very well been a doorway into realms of the spirit and dynamics of spiritual warfare that you have never considered. However, it is important that you and I understand that no matter what we know and what comes against us, we must maintain proper motives and character before the Lord. The heart of an intercessor is one that intervenes on behalf of others. It is very difficult to find a man called by God executing his own vengeance and obtaining vindication on his own behalf. Today I ask you to join the company of great men and women of God who have gone before us as intercessors and spiritual warriors. There is a great cloud of witnesses surrounding and beholding your Christlikeness; they celebrate the Lamb of God for what He has done in your life and will continue to do in your heart.

If you are a Christian then you are an intercessor. It is the basic duty of a priest. This book should have better equipped you to deal with the oppositions to the kingdom of God in your life and the powers that hold your loved ones captive in a more effective way. May you have good success as you lose nothing that you have learned through this book and apply these wonderful principles to the way you live life before God and establish His dominion in the heavens and the earth.

ABOUT THE AUTHOR

Brian D. Echevarria is loving, engaging, and intense. He is personable with a microphone and in his adventurous everyday life. He is a wholly given, laid down lover of Jesus and lives an uncompromising message of sacrifice and dedication. He preaches the Word of God with energy and unmistakable conviction while making no apologies for being radical and completely unbalanced when it comes to serving Jesus. As a servant of Jesus Christ, being commissioned to the nations where he brings the power of God with great force to break the power and sway of the enemy, Brian is establishing works for the Lord amongst the poor and training believers to be like Christ in personal holiness and as warriors establishing the Kingdom of God. As a visionary and a pioneer who steps out with faith and purpose, challenging others to believe God and pursue the vision that Jesus has given the Church, Brian is revolutionizing the way things are approached and done.

Brian D. Echevarria lives anywhere that he believes the Lord will use him with his beautiful family.

INFORMATION

For your spiritual enrichment and advancement, please find more meetings, seminars, and ministries with Brian D. Echevarria:

Website: www.JLIConnect.com

Email: info@JLIConnect.com

Reach us through Social Networks At

Facebook: www.facebook.com/Echevarria144

Twitter: @Echevarria144

Please enjoy other books by Brian D. Echevarria:

- *The Death of a Saint*
- *Servant Lordship*
- *Why Give?*
- *Jesus the Person* – Coming Soon

NOTES

[i] Strong, J. (1984). *The New Strong's Exhaustive Concordance of the Bible.* Nashville: Thomas Nelson Publishers.

[ii] intercede. Dictionary, Encyclopedia and Thesaurus – The Free Dictionar. Random House Kernerman Webster's College Dictionary, October 13, 2013, http://www.thefreedictionary.com/ /dict.aspx?rd=1&word=intercede.

[iii] Strong, J. (1984). *The New Strong's Exhaustive Concordance of the Bible.* Nashville: Thomas Nelson Publishers.

[iv] Strong, J. (1984). *The New Strong's Exhaustive Concordance of the Bible.* Nashville: Thomas Nelson Publishers.

Made in the USA
Charleston, SC
18 October 2013